YOU
HAVE BECOME
QUITE SPECIAL
TO ME

Poems for Lovers...by Lovers

The C. R. Gibson Company
Norwalk, Connecticut

For Diane,
      Dennis

To Dennis,
      Diane

I'd almost stopped
looking for
magic
or
asking for
miracles
and maybe
"stopping"
is the
secret
for you appeared the
moment
I
reached the
edge of
believing in
love
again.

I know not how to love again,
and no love waits for me.
Windy nights like these,
lost love is tossing through the trees.

But, there is "someone," I've been told,
who shall love me well enough.
And I will fall again through the rooftops
of the city of love.
To crash a party of one.

Lost races
remain in the
shadows
past fears
constantly
intrude
reminding us of
love's bitter
memories
in games we've
played
before.

*I*f I don't try to search.
Then I will find "you" by surprise.
Someday.

Where are you?
Around the next corner?
In a year or two?

I will know you.

I want to be in love again,
with all the feelings rushing through me.

Hesitation is like the pane of a window.
You can see me clearly
but cannot touch what lies beyond.

Why do I hold back?

Meeting you
touching you
and
sharing warm
feelings and a
time
with you...

Your gentleness is
sometimes painful
because I fear
it won't be
permanent.

I am the one who smiles
(a little too much)
And laughs at the jokes
(funny or not)
And shakes the hand
(too eagerly)
To compensate
for the wasted years
Spent in shyness,
Past hurt's surrender.

*F*reedom, care, touching,
time by myself.
Thinking of you.

You spin my head.
Your feelings toward me
turn my world around.

I think I fear
my soul opening,
my heart's caring.
The rollercoaster ride
to the brink.

*Wait for me!
to catch up to you
for your love...*

I went to a housewarming.
Solitary.
Didn't ask anyone to go with me.
I like to meet new people.

My friend the host had mentioned
the quiet person who lived upstairs.
Someone seldom seen.

I saw you from afar.
You were beautiful.
The way you filled your shirt
to shape the picture of Fleetwood Mac.
And the light catching at your hair,
an aura around the rich night of you.

You were waiting in the kitchen,
full of unspoken words, impossible dreams.
Some miracles quietly happen.
We went upstairs to where you lived
but I never met the hermit.
Although some say she was you.

Losing is a part of
living
an unfortunate
fate
for all
accepting a loss
gracefully
is a trait
acquired through
time
losing you may be
inevitable
(though not desired)
so give me
today
all of your
tomorrows.

I've lost myself
several times today...

I should be working
instead I'm thinking
of you
us
our image together:
>   laughing
>   sharing
>   understanding
>   &
>   giving
of
ourselves

...and it's hard to come back.

Each encounter surpasses expectations
beautiful and ultramundane.
Unspoken words conveyed by glances
through eyes of one whose response is the same.

Whether brief or long lasting, these
interludes will be:

remembered always,
cherished deeply.

You have become quite special to me.

I guess quietly is how
It begins . . .
Learning to trust again.

The past: so much
Deception and deceit.
Forgiving and being forgiven.
You are honest
And you understand

First times still
Surprise me

So many discoveries
That I can only
Flow onward
Amazed.

Occasionally
I
expect more from
you
than you are
able
to give...

allow me
time
to remember
that my
needs
are not
always
necessarily
yours.

No, never has
Anyone become
What you are to me.

And I am surprised.
Me, the walking wounded,
With a trail of tales
And slightly battered heart,
Being mended with love by you.

You have been
running
for so
long...
would you
like to
rest
for a while
in my
arms...

*T*he depth of your love
Is more than I can fathom.
But I am learning to breathe deeply,
I cannot drown in your peaceful ocean.
Cradle me as I change.

The past cannot hurt
cannot touch us
together
we're special —
don't run from me
give me the love
you
need so badly to
give
let it
surround me
for
I know
your love is
special
and I'll
hold it
softly
with care.

*T*his wild journey to the stars,
Love's realm in inner space.
Where everything is ours
As we whisper of the place.

As daring as the pioneers,
Charting new paths once we start.
Winding past old fears
And into new lands of the heart.

*B*rown your eyes,
Warm and dark
Electric hair afire.
And laughing.

Diane.

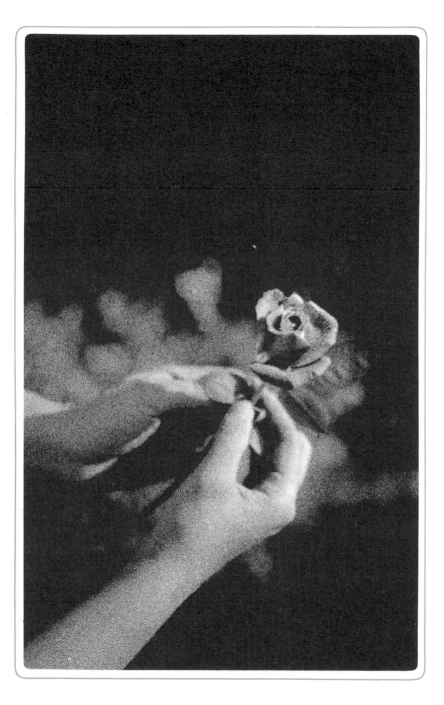

There is no hesitation for me now.
I don't hide my face or close my
eyes when I speak.

Though I still grow weak from your touch,
my words flow freely and are given without
fear of what tomorrow will bring.

Each time we meet there is something new.
We are stepping into a new land of words,
actions and feelings.

A beginning that we can explore and enjoy
together.

When I was four years old
Someone special was born.
(The grown-ups looked on
As I drew big pictures,
Some were as long as shelf paper.)

Where were you
When I was eight years old?
What were you doing at four?
Did you sing little songs
And play little games?

When we were fourteen/eighteen,
Why didn't we know what waited for us?
The world was too young, not ready.

I want a time machine,
So I can visit
All those other yous.

In a world full of
dreams
we
have found a
place
existing in a
second
space
of
magic
captured
in
each
other's
love.

Finally came together for
us
it clicked into place
the night
you let yourself slip
from the tightrope
and fell to
me
completely trusting
this time...
trusting me
not to hurt you
and feeling safe

       it's good
       that at last
       you've learned
       to fall
       without the
       pain.

Your world
My world
Ours together

Your eyes
And mine
Mingling

Our hearts
signaling
Caution, Care
For the tenderness
Already there
Loving loving
Cherishing
What we share.

You reside herein.
Thoughts of you come forth
To make me shake my head
And wonder,
The luck of me
To have these moments
Filled with you.

You have taken
time in your life...

shedding your past
at my
doorsteps
allowing yourself
to love
and be
loved
and bringing
only the
you
now

...for me.

*L*ove is my shelter
Your arms are my home.
I wish I were there
But, I'm here, missing you.

The telephone allows me
Only your voice.

So, I'll imagine your eyes
Looking into mine
And fall into them like
Alice fell into Wonderland.

Until we are together again.

Seldom do you encounter a person willing
to give themselves totally to another
even
for
a
day
an
hour
a minute.

The times we've shared are appreciated.

You were standing there
As I drove away.
I kept your image
In my rear view mirror
And didn't let it fade.

That morning thoughts of you
Were filed safely away
In the folders of my mind . . .

But are we ready for another wide week
of days apart but for the touch
of our love?

Your smiles are bright bookmarks
between the leaves of my life.

You have gone...

but
thoughts
of you
linger
so I can recapture
past
serenity
that we
have passed through
in
our
time alone —
together

...and I feel your presence
long after you have gone.

I cannot speak when
you hold me...

I can only glide through
the infinite space
leading to your eyes
where I become
hopelessly lost...

*L*oving you
Is no more spectacular
Than diving into a cloud.

I get no more excited
Than a whirling dervish,
And you hold me hardly twice as
Close as a mother holds her child.

I will love you
for as long
as you
give to me
your
smile.

Written by Diane Strayhorn
and Dennis Hejduk

Set in Perpetua Italic
and Palatino

Designed by Thomas James Aaron